To all the invisible disability warriors, your illness may not be visible, but your strength is powerful.

To my Mum and Dad, thank you for your endless love, patience, support and belief in me, especially on the days I didn't believe in myself. I love you.

To Meg from Helpful Hounds, thank you for your unwavering belief in both Bonnie and I. Thank you for helping her become the incredible helper and dog I never knew I would need.

To my Bonnie, thank you for being brave, being my shadow, my steady paws, my reminder that loves goes beyond words.

This is our story.

BONNIE THE BRAVE

A Service Dog Story

I was born with many brothers and sisters; it was a nice warm wriggly pile of puppies.

They love to snooze, eat and play all day.

But me?

I like to watch and listen.

I know I am different to my siblings; I have a super special job to do.

I just do not know what that job is yet.

One afternoon I was playing chase and catch with my brothers and sisters.

A car arrives.

A new human is here. She moves really slowly and has two bright shiny sticks under her arms.

She does not say a word, but I can see something in her eyes.

My ears prick up, my heart whispers, "it's her!"

I do not wait a second longer.

I run straight over and climb into her lap.

I found my human, my reason for being here, my job.

I do not want to leave her lap.

I can feel that something in her body is different to the other humans I know.

Even her legs do not move like other humans, she uses the shiny sticks to walk, but I do not mind.

If I keep snuggling up to her, she will know that it is okay to rest.

I understand now, she needs me in a way no one else ever has.

I am learning that sometimes my human's body does not do the things she wants it to do.

Sometimes her legs stop working.

She takes naps in strange places.

Sometimes she goes very quiet.

Other people look worried, but me, I stay close.

I watch, I listen and I snuggle her.

I am starting to notice tiny things.

She starts to breathe slowly, her eyes look funny.

Oh there she goes, she is taking another nap.

This is my super important job; I am going to keep her safe.

Today I meet a new friend. This new human has arrived and I instantly like her; she has brought me many yummy snacks and toys to play with.

My new friend sits and watches me carefully as I stay close to my human.

"Bonnie" she says, "you are a smart girl. Let's train you to be an even better helper."

My ears flick together, and my tail wags, "a helper, a service dog?"

My new friend is teaching me so many tricks; to sit, stay, touch.

I think my favourite thing she is teaching me is how to help when my human's body gets a bit wobbly.

As we are learning these tricks my human is very still. Her head is dropping, she is not answering.

I am a little confused. I have so many things to try and remember.

Wait, nudge her with my nose, bark once, lay down on her legs.

My human's fingers move and she has taken a breath again.

"Yessssss, I did it!"

Z
Z
Z
z

Today my friend is back, and she has a special vest for me.

She said we are going on an adventure.

My jacket is so cool - it's green and says:

'Service Dog In Training'.

It means I am still learning so I can make mistakes.

SERVICE DOG IN TRAINING
HELPFUL HOUNDS

My human is coming too.

I must remember to sit, not ask for any of her food, watch her, wait and make sure I am ready to help her if she takes a nap on the ground.

TRAIL 518 A
TRAIL 518

Gosh I have come a long way since I was a wriggly little jelly-bean with my brothers and sisters.

But guess what:

I am still learning,

some days I get it right,

some days I forget,

but my human and I, we are a team.

We practice in parks, cafes, and shops.

If you see me out with my vest, please do not say hi to me.

I will want to be your friend, but it is important I focus on my human.

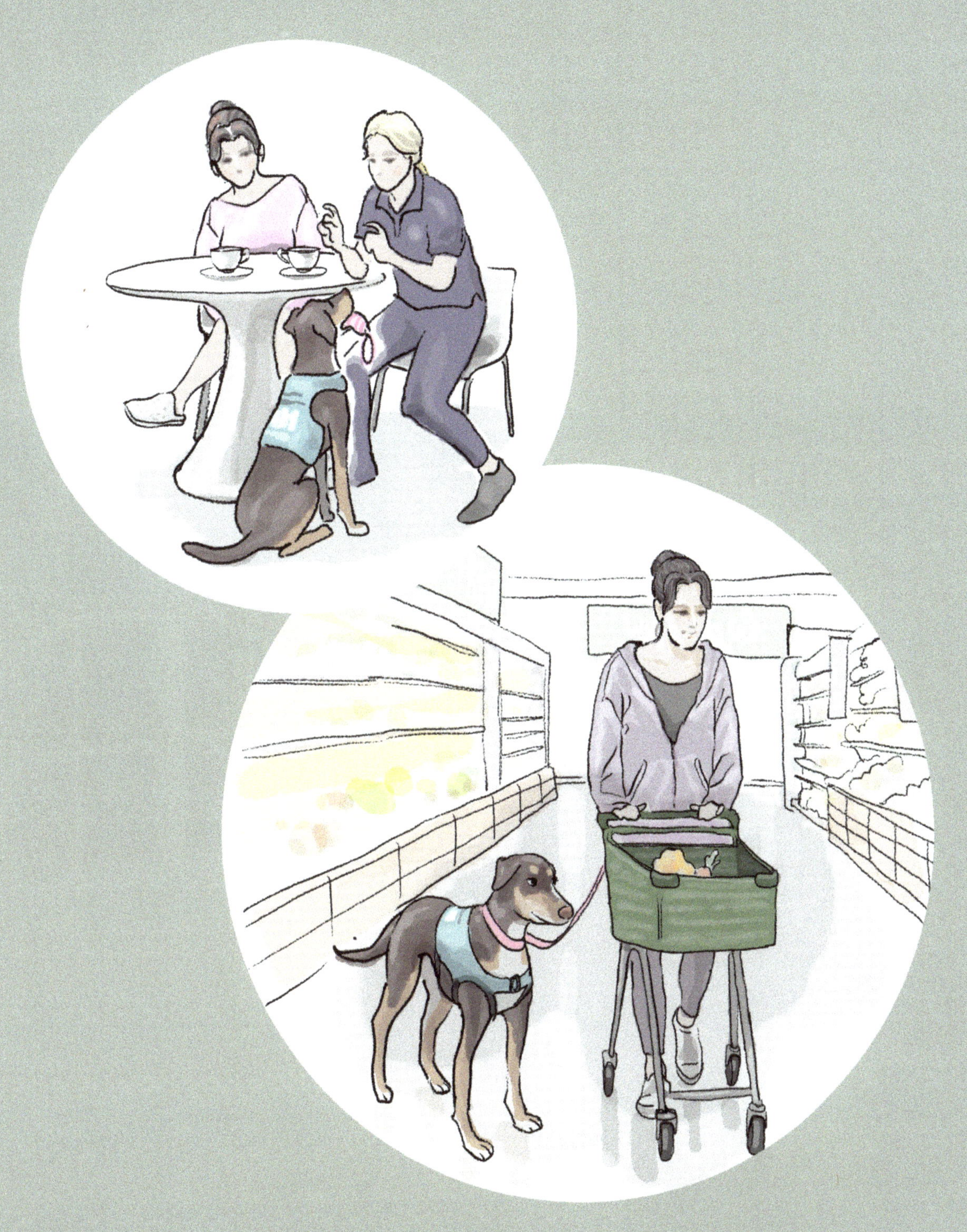

When the day ends
and the stars shine
bright, I curl up next
to my human.

She does not need
to say a word.

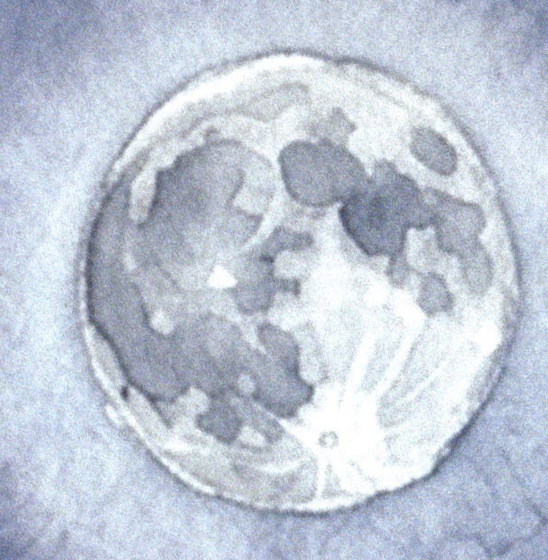

Some people cannot see what she lives with, but I see and feel it everyday.

I can feel her love and she can feel mine.

I do not know why her body does different things, but I am proud to be her helper.

From the Author:

Hi, I'm Elsie, Bonnie's real life human. This story is based on our journey together, as we learn and grow and face each day. In 2024, I was diagnosed with a condition called Functional Neurological Disorder, (FND). It affects how my brain and body work together.

It can cause many different symptoms, that include weakness in my limbs, seizures, tremors and ticks, speech difficulty, just to name a few.

Most of the time I "look fine" but my body is fighting against itself. This is where Bonnie comes in.

Bonnie is training to be a service dog. She isn't just a puppy or a companion. She is my partner and my everyday helper. With the help of a trainer, she is learning how to keep me safe when my symptoms affect me and my body. She is learning to support me in a world that isn't always easy to navigate with a disability.

I wrote this story to help kids and adults to understand that not all disabilities are visible. It's a reminder that some dogs are working and mustn't be interacted with while they are doing their very important job. Support, love and teamwork comes in all forms, even from four-legged companions.

Thank you for reading our story. If you live with an invisible disability, or love someone who suffers from one, or are just learning, please know, we appreciate your support, we see you, we support you and you are not alone.

Big Love, Elsie and Bonnie.

Photo: Thomas Donoghoe

About FND:

Functional Neurological Disorder (FND) is a neurological condition that affects how the brain and the body work together. It causes neurological symptoms without causing any damage to the brain. Approximately 21,500 people in Australia are living with FND.

Living with FND can be confusing, frustrating and sometimes scary. The symptoms are very real but not always visible. Many people with FND have to learn how to manage their energy levels, their stress, their environment and their safety everyday.

It is a condition that affects everyone a little differently. Symptoms can vary depending on the person. Some symptoms include but are not limited to:

- Non-epileptic seizures or dissociative attacks.

- Limb weakness or paralysis, tremors and ticks.

- Slurred speak, difficulty speaking or finding words.

This is where service dogs can be a life changing tool for people suffering from FND or any invisible disability.

Learn more: www.fndaus.org.au

Service Dogs for people with Invisible Disabilities:

Service dogs are very special for people with disabilities. Each service dog is trained specifically for their human's needs. They are trained in specific tasks to offer support to their person, to help enhance their independence, safety and quality of life.

Some specific tasks Bonnie is trained for,
to support me on a daily basis include:

- Seizure alert and response.

- Mobility assistance.

- Deep pressure therapy.

- Alerting to change in heart rate.

- Providing grounding in an overwhelming situation.

Each service dog is trained to support their human in the way that is needed for them. Service dogs are an integral part of life for people with invisible disabilities, as they help us navigate a world that isn't always safe for us.